Ripley Readers

All true and unbelievable!

Learning to read. Reading to learn!

LEVEL ONE Sounding It Out Preschool–Kindergarten
For kids who know their alphabet and are starting to sound out words.

learning sight words • beginning reading • sounding out words

LEVEL TWO Reading with Help Preschool–Grade 1
For kids who know sight words and are learning to sound out new words.

expanding vocabulary • building confidence • sounding out bigger words

LEVEL THREE Independent Reading Grades 1–3
For kids who are beginning to read on their own.

introducing paragraphs • challenging vocabulary • reading for comprehension

LEVEL FOUR Chapters Grades 2–4
For confident readers who enjoy a mixture of images and story.

reading for learning • more complex content • feeding curiosity

Ripley Readers Designed to help kids build their reading skills and confidence at any level, this program offers a variety of fun, entertaining, and unbelievable topics to interest even the most reluctant readers. With stories and information that will spark their curiosity, each book will motivate them to start and keep reading.

Vice President, Licensing & Publishing Amanda Joiner
Editorial Manager Carrie Bolin

Editor Jessica Firpi
Writer Korynn Wible-Freels
Designer Scott Swanson
Reprographics Bob Prohaska
Production Design Luis Fuentes

Published by Ripley Publishing 2020

10 9 8 7 6 5 4 3 2 1

Copyright © 2020 Ripley Publishing

ISBN: 978-1-60991-403-5

No part of this publication may be reproduced in whole or in part, stored in a retrieval system, or transmitted in any form by any means, electronic, mechanical, photocopying, recording, or otherwise, without written permission from the publisher.

For more information regarding permission, contact:
VP Licensing & Publishing
Ripley Entertainment Inc.
7576 Kingspointe Parkway, Suite 188
Orlando, Florida 32819

Email: publishing@ripleys.com
www.ripleys.com/books
Manufactured in China in May 2020.

First Printing

Library of Congress Control Number: 2020936954

PUBLISHER'S NOTE
While every effort has been made to verify the accuracy of the entries in this book, the Publisher cannot be held responsible for any errors contained in the work. They would be glad to receive any information from readers.

PHOTO CREDITS
Cover © NaturesMomentsuk/Shutterstock **3** © NaturesMomentsuk/Shutterstock **4-5** © Scott E Read/Shutterstock **6-7** © Hung Chung Chih/Shutterstock **8-9** George Lepp via Getty Images **10-11** © Kelp Grizzly Photography/Shutterstock **12-13** © FloridaStock/Shutterstock **14-15** Mint Images/Art Wolfe via Getty Images **16-17** © Lamberrto/Shutterstock **18-19** © Adam Van Spronsen/Shutterstock **20-21** © PHOTO BY LOLA/Shutterstock **22-23** Paul Souders via Getty Images **24-25** © Jim Freeman/Shutterstock **26-27** Tarik Thami/EyeEm via Getty Images **28-29** Ian Mcallister via Getty Images **30-31** © PhotocechCZ/Shutterstock **Master Graphics** Created by Scott Swanson

All other photos are from Ripley Entertainment Inc. Every attempt has been made to acknowledge correctly and contact copyright holders and we apologize in advance for any unintentional errors or omissions, which will be corrected in future editions.

LEXILE®, LEXILE FRAMEWORK®, LEXILE ANALYZER®, the LEXILE® logo and POWERV® are trademarks of MetaMetrics, Inc., and are registered in the United States and abroad. The trademarks and names of other companies and products mentioned herein are the property of their respective owners. Copyright © 2020 MetaMetrics, Inc. All rights reserved.

Ripley Readers

Bears!

All true and unbelievable!

a Jim Pattison Company

Big claws! Big teeth! What can it be?

It is a bear!

Bears have black, brown, or white fur.

Look, this one has two colors!

Bears like honey, but they eat bugs, fish, and grass, too!

Wow!

A bear can run as fast as a horse!

 This bear wants to jump in the water.

Did you know many bears are good swimmers?

You can find bears all over the world!

There are eight kinds of bears.

How many can you name?

Not all bears go to sleep in the winter.

Pandas have a lot to eat all year!

A panda can eat 20 pounds of bamboo a day!

Polar bears are the biggest. They can stand almost as tall as a basketball hoop!

Look out, fish!

That polar bear can swim faster than the fastest human can!

Sun bears are little, but they are good at climbing up trees!

Did you know some black bears are white?

They are called spirit bears.

Sloth bears look funny with no front teeth!

These animals are bear-y cool!

# Ripley Readers

All true and unbelievable!

Ready for More?

Ripley Readers feature unbelievable but true facts and stories!

  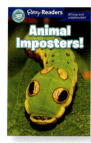 

For more information about Ripley's Believe It or Not!, go to www.ripleys.com